MEXICO CITY

The Cubby
2024 Long Weekend Guide

James Cubby

MEXICO CITY
The Cubby
Long Weekend Guide

TABLE OF CONTENTS

Chapter 1
WHY MEXICO CITY?

I love Mexico City, even though the first time I traveled there, with my mother, we almost brought her back in a box. She had made the mistake of using the ice cubes in her hotel room fridge to make a drink instead of pouring bottled water into the ice trays.

Boom!

You're sick as a dog.

But that was many years ago. Generally, I've had nothing but wonderful times in Mexico City.

When I think about what Mexico City was and how it came to be what it is today, my mind still boggles.

You must remember that the whole city is built on a drained lakebed. When there was still a lake, around 1325, it was established as the Aztec capital called Tenochititlán. The island in the middle of the lake was reached by way of a series of causeways. This was what Hernan Cortes found when he showed up in 1521. He promptly destroyed it.

Mexico has a rich and bloody history, not unlike all the other countries in the New World where the indigenous populations where slaughtered or enslaved. (But one must remember that Cortes didn't do anything to the Aztecs that the English settlers didn't do to the Indians.)

The altitude is high, over 7,000 feet, so if you come from a low-lying coastal area, be prepared for some difficulty in breathing. And while the government has made enormous strides in cleaning up the famously polluted air in Mexico City, it's still awful. You must pray for good air. But you can never be sure of it.

There are things about Mexico in general that you want to be aware of if you want to travel wisely—and safely. The State Department says 14 of the 31 states (and Federal District, or *Distrito Federal*, or D.F., which is Mexico City) have no travel warnings. The others you want to avoid because of the drug-related gang warfare that's an ongoing reality in Mexico, responsible for ripping the country apart. (Americans are really to blame since we're the ones buying all the drugs.)

One of the reasons Mexico City is so much more safe than other parts of the country is that everybody wants to be able to come here and visit it in peace, and this includes a lot of the high-end drug dealers, many of whom have houses and families here. They don't want to come here and duel it out on the streets the way they do elsewhere.

Of the 20 top foreign locations for Americans, 4 are in Mexico: No. 2 is Cancun, followed by No. 3, Playa del Carmen, Cabo san Lucas / Los Cabos at No. 11 and Puerto Vallarta at No. 15.

One good thing about Mexico City is that it has been sidestepped by the drug cartels so there's no sense of the overwhelming violence that occurs in other parts of Mexico.

You will find the *Distrito Federal* (Federal District, another name for the city) to be quite a beautiful, handsomely laid-out city.

Lay of the Land

At 571 square miles, D.F.—as Mexico City residents, or *chilangos*, call it—is vast, but visitors gravitate to a few key neighborhoods.

Centro Histórico: Anchored by the Zócalo plaza, the historic center is a mix of monuments and bustling commerce.

Roma: Hipsters, artists, and boutique owners have revived this once-bourgeois neighborhood of Art Nouveau mansions.

Condesa: In Mexico City's answer to New York's West Village, shops, restaurants, and apartments radiate out from the Parque México.

Polanco: One of the city's poshest districts keeps expanding north: "Nuevo Polanco" is being colonized by galleries and shopping malls.

Getting Around Safely: Taxis are plentiful, but you may feel more secure having a private car. From Journey Mexico at www.journeymexico.com

For the latest safety information, go to the U.S. State Department at travel.state.gov.

CASH & DEBIT CARDS.

Notify the companies whose cards you use that you are going to Mexico. Transactions might be blocked if you don't. Have them send you alerts or call you if any charge looks suspicious. When using ATMs, try to avoid street side ATMs in favor of ATMS inside a bank or other business.

Have credit card numbers and other information written down in a safe place.

You'll need cash because a lot of places don't accept plastic. But get your currency converted before going to Mexico because you'll stick out as a foreigner by getting it done at the airport when you land. (The rates are high there too.) A lot of currency exchange booths are not in secure areas, so beware.

YOUR DRESS.

You're not in Vegas, you're in a potentially dangerous city, so leave the shorts and flip-flops at home unless you're visiting the beach somewhere. Don't be an obvious tourist. Keep your camera in your travel bag, not around your neck.

YOUR PHONE.

Don't be glued to it the way so many people are, not when you're out on the streets. You're begging for trouble.

Check with your carrier to find out what the fees are when traveling in Mexico.

Chapter 2
GETTING ABOUT

UBER
https://www.uber.com/global/en/cities/mexico-city/

Helpful tips from Uber

There's an extensive Metro system, a bus system, a trolley system. I would avoid them all unless you *really* know your way around. I never use them. Never.

They even have special cars on the Metro system for women only because women get groped on the mixed cars. Also, there's the constant threat of pickpockets. Stay away.

Mexico City is one of the world's largest cities and boasts an estimated population of 21 million people living in the region. Mexico City is divided into 16 areas known as delegaciones, not unlike New York's boroughs. These areas are further divided into neighborhoods called "colonias" and there are about 250 of these.

When traveling the city, it is important to know which colonia that you're traveling to and be aware that some have duplicate or very similar names. Visitors to Mexico City need to take note of the increase in crime and safety concerns that are prevalent in the city.

While traveling throughout Mexico City by public transportation can be economical, it is not always the safest mode of transportation and warnings regarding use of public transportation should be respected.

Locals and those familiar with Mexico City travel freely and cheaply via the Metro, first- and second-class buses.

However, visitors should travel by **sitio taxis** (official taxis registered to a specific locale or hotel), as these taxis are inexpensive and the safest means of travel within the city.

"Turismo" and Sitio Taxis

These two methods are the safest means of travel within Mexico City. Turismo taxis, un-marked cabs, are usually luxury cars that are assigned to specific hotels and are identified by their special license plates. These may be more expensive that other taxis but they are the safest.

Established rates are fixed for travel to and from the airport. However, rates for traveling to other destinations and sightseeing need to be negotiated with the drivers.

The bell captain at your hotel can tell you what the airport fare should be and make sure to confirm with the cab driver before departure. Theses cab drivers, usually licensed English-speaking guides, can be excellent tour guides and provide valuable information regarding Mexico City.

While these cabs usually charge around 15% more than metered rates, the price is well worth it as these drivers can wait for you while you dine or shop or will pick you up when you call.

Getting Around Safely: Taxis are plentiful, but you may feel more secure having a private car. From Journey Mexico at <u>www.journeymexico.com</u>

Metered Taxis

Some sitio taxis (radio taxis) are safe and use meters, others have fixed rates. Travelers need to be cautious as some drivers will overcharge passengers, advance the meter, or even drive farther than requested to run up the tab.

Do not hail a taxi. A lot of the drivers are unlicensed, illegal and unsafe.

Your hotel will call a reputable taxi for you, a "radio taxi." If you're in a restaurant and ready to leave at night, have them call a cab for you.

If you're out on the street and need a cab, go into a nearby hotel or restaurant and have them call for you. Or go to a taxi stand, labeled *Sitio de Taxi,* where real taxis will be located. These are designated taxis and OK to use. These maroon and gold Nissans are slightly more expensive than the green *libre* taxis, but much more secure.

Metro

The Mexico City subway offers one of the cheapest fares in the world and has twelve lines that cover the entire city. The Metro is open Monday – Friday (5 a.m. to midnight), Saturday (6 a.m. to midnight), and Sunday (7 a.m. to midnight). The

Metro is very crowded during the day and traveling during rush hours should be avoided. Tickets are sold at the ticket booth in each station. After passing through the turnstile, look for two large signs showing the destinations and follow the signs. Make sure you know where you are going as there is only one map with the routes at the entrance of the station. Note: SALIDA means EXIT and ANDENES means PLATFORMS. Once you get on the train, there's a map of the station stops for that line only located above each door. CORRESPONDENCIAS means transfer points. Be prepared to walk a bit inside the Metro system, especially when transferring lines. **Remember, this is not the safest way to travel and Metro pickpockets prey on tourists.**

Bus

Traveling by bus is common for locals. However, visitors should beware. There are bus stops on all the major tourist streets and most post a map with the full route description. The Metrobus, introduced in 2006, runs in its own designated lane up and down Avenida Insurgentes and usually travels faster than the surrounding traffic. Most of these buses are used by commuters but if you know where you're going and know the stop, the Metrobus is a better alternative to the other buses.

Microbuses

Some tourists like to use the peseros (microbuses); these are sedans or minibuses that run along major roadways. These buses have established fares and pick up and let off passengers along the route and usually offer a more comfortable ride and speedy journey. These microbuses are usually green and gray and display cards in the windshield with their routes. As the bus nears a stop, the driver will put his hand out the wind displaying one or more fingers indicating the number of passengers he can accommodate.

Tourist Bus

Many cities feature the red double-decker hop-on and hop-off tour buses (in Mexico City they are called **Turibuses;** www.turibus.com.mx and here in Mexico City they offer different tours in the north and south of the city. Each bus seats 75 and offers an audio tour in five languages. These buses operate from 9 a.m. to 9 p.m. and for a set fee tourists can hop-on and hop off as often as desired. One of their most popular tours is the Chapultepec-Centro

Histórico route with 25 stops including major monuments, museums and neighborhoods. Another favorite circuit takes passengers from La Roma neighborhood south with stops that include the World Trade Center, Plaza de Torros bullring, Carillo Gil museum, Perisur shopping center, and the Frida Kahlo Museum. Another tour route goes to the pyramids at Teotihuacán.

Rental Car

If you are traveling without a car and want to travel to Puebla or other surrounding areas, you may consider a rental car. Be warned that due to the high percentage of auto theft, **renting a car in Mexico City is not recommended**.

Do not rent a car unless you're familiar with the area. These people drive like maniacs. The last thing you want is to be in a fender bender in this country where bribes are so common. If you're not prepared to deal with the police, avoid renting a car.

It is not advised to drive in the city if you're not familiar with the streets and neighborhoods, especially if you don't read Spanish, as all the signs are in Spanish, and you certainly don't want to take the chance of landing in one of the city's unsavory neighborhoods. One safe option is to hire a car with a driver—Avis offers chauffeur-driven rental cars at all its Mexico City locations –the drivers know the area and are great tour guides. (Avis – 800-352-7900 in the U.S. or 1-800-288-8888 in Mexico).

HOTEL

CONDESA DF
Avenue Veracruz 102, Col., 52 55 5241-2600
www.condesadf.com/main.html
NEIGHBORHOOD: Condesa
This is one of the top places you will want to consider
staying in because it's new and hip and attracts a
trendy crowd not only as guests, but to its charming
public spaces. Paris designer India Mahdavi took over
this 1920s French Neoclassical style building and

jumped it up with turquoise walls and ultra-modern furnishings. The outside of the building is distinguished and stately. Inside, it's a crazy wonderful colorful surprise. They offer 40 rooms arrayed around a courtyard in the center. The place is decorated with alpaca carpets, Oaxacan blankets, dark wood paneling and other fun items. The Condesa neighborhood is home to numerous art galleries and fun, stimulating shops, so this place also makes an excellent stop for a drink after you've done some exploring and shopping. (Get the cucumber mezcal mojito made with mezcal blanco by Los Danzantes of Oaxaca.) If you're visiting in the spring, you'll love the blooming jacaranda trees with purple flowers surrounding the rooftop terrace where there's also a sushi bar. In the basement at night there's a dance club where it goes on till late.

DOWNTOWN MEXICO HOTEL
Isabel La Católica 30, Mexico City, +52 55 5130 6830
www.downtownmexico.com
NEIGHBORHOOD: Downtown/Historical District
This hotel combines Colonial 17th century grandeur with a modern twist. Next to Colonial landmarks on a cobbled street, this hotel is in the central balcony of the Palace of the Countess of Miravalle. In a unique setting filled with art, guests can enjoy breakfast. The large terrace offers great views of the historic churches, Torre Latinoamericana and the Casino Espanol. The owners, Grupo Habita, have elegantly combined the old structure with modern touches, like the bar and pool on the rooftop that attracts a fun

crowd. Be sure to explore the mezzanine where there are carefully selected shops selling mescal, pottery from the provinces and rich chocolates. Amenities include Flat screen TVs, Bigelow Apothecaries, dry cleaning, Wi-Fi, and room service.

FOUR SEASONS HOTEL MEXICO, D.F.
Paseo de la Reforma 500, Mexico City, +52 55 5230 1818
www.fourseasons.com/mexico/
NEIGHBORHOOD: Cuauhtémoc
Located near Chapultepec Park, this beautiful hotel has a staff as smooth as any you'll find in any Four Seasons hotel around the world. You get the feel of colonial times in the lobby and rooms, as well as the courtyard, its fountain offering a soothing respite from the din outside. The hotel offers 240 elegantly appointed guest rooms, including 40 suites. Amenities include LCD flat-screen TVs, free wireless high-

speed Internet access, heated outdoor pool, spa, and fitness center. On-site restaurant, **Reforma 500**, offers Latin American cuisine and lunch and/or cocktails are available at **El Bar**. Around the corner from the hotel entrance, on Calle Burdeos, you'll find street-side vendors selling good tacos and other street food.

INTERCONTINENTAL PRESIDENTE MEXICO CITY
Campos Elíseos 218, Polanco, Polanco IV Secc, 11560 Ciudad de México, CDMX, +52 55 5327 7700
www.ihg.com/intercontinental/hotels/gb/en/reservation
NEIGHBORHOOD: Federal District / Polanco
Overlooking Chapultepec Park, this modern high-rise (42 floors) hotel offers 661 guest rooms and suites. From the higher floors you get a magnificent view of the mountains that encircle the city (when the air isn't terribly polluted, which is not often). Depending on your rate, you'll probably get a buffet breakfast included with your room. You'll find it to be heads and shoulders above most such buffets, with eggs made to order, lots of pastries. There are 5 or 6 restaurants on site, including an outpost of New York's steakhouse, the **Palm**, **Chapulin** (serving Mexican cuisine), an import from Paris, the bistro **Au Pied de Cochon**, which actually does a great job of replicating the bistro atmosphere they have in Paris; the trattoria **Alfredo di Roma**, that has a nice outdoor terrace. Once I was here on a whirlwind 4-day trip working on a movie script and the producers put me up here. I was holed up, never able to leave the room

except occasionally. I spent time in all these restaurants and was very satisfied. Amenities: Wi-Fi (surcharge), flat-screen TVs, iPod docks and coffeemakers. Hotel facilities: cocktail lounge, health club & spa, ballroom, and indoor swimming pool. Conveniently located near National Museum of Anthropology, Ruth Lechuga Museum and Paseo de la Reforma, which has lots of buses and numerous cabs.

LA CASONA
Durango 280, Cuauhtémoc, Mexico City, +52 55 5286 3001
https://la-casona.hotels-mexico-city.com/
NEIGHBORHOOD: Federal District
With its central location, this small, cozy hotel offers guests 29 exclusive guest rooms. Amenities include

free 10Mb Fibreoptic Internet, flat screen TV with cable, safe deposit boxes, writing desk, room service, air conditioning, and snack basket. No smoking rooms available. Facilities include Restaurant, bar, reading room, gymnasium and steam room. Bicycles available for guests.

LA VALISE
Tonalá 53, Mexico City, 386-301-4831
www.lavalise.com
NEIGHBORHOOD: Roma
Probably the hottest, hippest place in all Mexico City is Roma, loaded with shops, restaurants and bars, but few hotels. However, there's a great little lodging owned by French ex-patriot designer Emmanuel Picault, who opened a few rooms above his distinctive shop in a building dating back to the 1920s on a street lined with trees. Picault, originally from

Normandy, has designed interiors for the local **Chic by Accident** (a trendy shop) and a local nightclub, **M. N. Roy** (in a subterranean space behind a rundown ice cream parlor, also in Roma), as well as Nüba, one of the better nightclubs in Paris. The décor in the 3 rooms he offers for rent here are very modern but reflect his appreciation of Mesoamerican art of the Mayans and Aztecs. There's a hammock strung up in the atrium, adding a whimsical touch. Each of the 3 suites offer different takes on black-and-white, while the outside of the building reflects an ornate Beaux-Arts look. There's no restaurant, but one of the best restaurants in the city is nearby, **Rosetta**, and waiters will come over with breakfast, lunch or dinner if you ask them.

LAS ALCOBAS
Presidente Masaryk 390, Mexico City, +52 55 3300 3900
www.lasalcobas.com
NEIGHBORHOOD: Federal District

Located in one of the most exclusive neighborhoods of Mexico City, his masterfully designed boutique hotel offers 35 guest rooms, suites and penthouses. Most of the residences offer wraparound terraces and all feature state of the art technology. The hotel features in room spa facilities, rain showers, and Jacuzzi. Facilities include on-site restaurant and spa.

LIVE AQUA BOSQUES
Paseo de Los Tamarindos 98, Mexico City, +52 443 137 8728
www.liveaqua.com
NEIGHBORHOOD: Bosques de las Lomas
This unique and innovative hotel offers a relaxed ambiance in a luxury setting. Now, bear in mind that it's about an hour outside downtown in the Santa Fe neighborhood, but it attracts a good clientele. The hotel offers 114 luxurious guest rooms and 23 suites. Amenities include: 46-inch Smart TV, Nespresso

coffeemaker, and motorized drapes. Every floor has its own concierge. On-site restaurant and Spa.

RED TREE HOUSE

Culiacan 6, Mexico City, +52 55 5584 3829
www.theredtreehouse.com
NEIGHBORHOOD: Federal District
This is Mexico City's top B&B. You'll get personal service and lots of hospitality. This is not a luxury hotel but the rooms are tasteful with beautiful surroundings. Amenities include free wireless Internet and a free breakfast. Conveniently located near parks, restaurants, art galleries, shopping, and city transportation.

ST REGIS

Paseo de la Reforma 439, Mexico City, 52 55 5228 1818
https://www.marriott.com/en-us/hotels/mexxr-the-st-regis-mexico-city
NEIGHBORHOOD: Cuauhtemoc

Located in the first 15 floors of the sleek, 31-story
Torre Libertad (designed by Cesar Pelli), the St.
Regis Mexico City overlooks the Paseo de la

Reforma. The luxury hotel offers 189 large and very
plush rooms, including 36 suites and a grand
presidential suite. Amenities include: Remede bath
amenities, GDA system for master control, oversized
flat screen TVs, CD/DVD player, and in-room digital
movie system. Wi-Fi Internet Access available. Hotel
facilities include King Cole Bar and a Spa and Fitness
Center from which there happens to be one of the best
views in the whole city.

**St Regis (center above) and the
King Cole Bar (below)**

Chapter 4
WHERE TO EAT

One good thing about eating in Mexico City is that it's possible to eat cheaply here from one end of town to the other. The street food is terrific, maybe the best in the world except for certain cities in Southeast Asia. Every corner will have great food on it.

TOURS-FOOD
CLUB TENGO HAMBRE
https://clubtengohambre.com/
If you find exploring the fascinating topic of Mexican cuisine a little on the daunting side, you won't be the first one to grapple with some basic fears. Should I drink the water? (Only if it's bottled.) Should I eat the food? This latter question is especially pertinent when it comes to the famous "street food" one finds on

every corner in this sprawling city. A great way to deal with this, and have some fun as well, is to take one of the tours offered by this company. You'll have some wonderful experiences, and you won't be afraid to eat the food. Besides the food, you'll get an insider's guide to the city.

MEXICO CITY STREET FOOD ESSENTIALS
This walking tour takes about 3 ½ hours and makes 6 stops. They insist the places they stop to eat will serve food only available here in the city, and not in other places in the country. Interesting, right?

INSIDER'S GUIDE TO MEXICO CITY'S STREET FOOD – MARKETS + SWEETS + PULQUE
This walking tour takes between 3 and 4 hours and makes 6 stops.
With this tour, they take you to the best & most interestingly varied food stands downtown, as well as markets, panaderias, confectioneries, and introduce you to pulque, which is a milk-colored drink that goes back centuries and packs a real punch. It's the fermented juice of the maguey plant (the agave plant—the blue agave is used to make tequila). It looks somewhat off-putting (even disgusting), but after the second one, you'll grow to love it. LOL.

MEXICO CITY AFTER DARK
This walking tour takes about 3 ½ hours and makes 7 stops. I really enjoyed this one, because I don't like to go out too late by myself, but this was great fun.

Some food stands are best at night, and I've never had better tacos, anywhere, period. They also take you to an historic cantina and a pulqueria where you can really get soused.

AMAYA
Calle Gral. Prim 95, +01 55 5592 5671
http://www.amayamexico.com/
CUISINE: International
DRINKS: Full Bar
SERVING: Lunch & Dinner
PRICE RANGE: $$$
NEIGHBORHOOD: Juárez
Lovely little place with high ceilings and Aztec / Mayan murals painted over old red brick walls that give the eatery a certain charm. A small bar has a handful of seats where you can also eat. Small but complex menu featuring dishes like: Lamp pita, Soft

shell crab, and Tuna ceviche. Nice wine list focusing on natural wines. Excellent Vegetarian options.

AZUL CONDESA
Nuevo León 68, Cuauhtémoc, Hipódromo, Mexico City, +52-55-5286-6380
www.azul.rest
CUISINE: Mexican
DRINKS: Full Bar
SERVING: Breakfast, Lunch
PRICE RANGE: $$$
NEIGHBORHOOD: Condesa
Chef Ricardo Munoz Zurita offers a menu of authentic Mexican cuisine in a simple atmosphere of wooden tables and chairs. Though the dining room is electric with activity, try to get one of the tables in the atrium garden if you can swing it. Very lush and tropical. Menu favorites include Beef drizzled in a smoky Oaxacan mole, Veracruz style fish, and

ancient Mayan dishes. Try the "enigmatico" chichilo negro, which is one of the 7 Oaxaca moles you seldom see. (It's made with chihuacle pepper ashes and is usually served with beef.)

AZUL HISTÓRICO

Isabel la Católica, 30, Centro Historico A, 52 55 5510 1316
www.azul.rest
CUISINE: Mexican
DRINKS: Full Bar
SERVING: Brunch, Lunch, Dinner
PRICE RANGE: $$$
NEIGHBORHOOD: Downtown south / Centro Sur
With lights in the thick-branched trees overhead, you couldn't find a more romantic spot than this popular restaurant serving favorites like Stuffed Duck Fritters dipped in mole and Black Chichilo Chiluacle Chili served with venison. This is also a great place for breakfast, serving favorites like chilaquiles, Mexican eggs, and enchiladas. Try the delicious house-made chocolate cake served with gorgonzola cheese ice cream.

BELMONDO

Tabasco 109, Mexico City, +55 62 73 2079
http://belmondo.mx/
DRINKS: Wines
SERVING: Lunch & Dinner
PRICE RANGE: $
NEIGHBORHOOD: Roma Norte
This eatery draws lots of young creative and trendy
types and offers a simple menu featuring salads,
sandwiches as spot on and good as any you've had
anywhere. Also, a curated list of wines by the glass.
Menu favorites include: the French dip with roast
beef and gravy, or the grilled cheese with caramelized
onions. Closed Sundays. Be prepared for a wait.

BÓSFORO
Luis Moya 31, Mexico City, +52 55 5512 1991
No Website
CUISINE: Mexican
DRINKS: Full Bar
SERVING: Breakfast, Lunch, Dinner
PRICE RANGE: $$
NEIGHBORHOOD: Federal District
This small friendly neighborhood bar specializes in
mezcales and offers a menu of Mexican bar food with
favorites like the quesadilla and tapas. Try the
desserts especially if you're a chocolate lover.

CABRERA 7
Calle Plaza Luis Cabrera 7, Miguel Hidalgo, Mexico
City, 52 55 5264 4465
CUISINE: Mexican

DRINKS: Full Bar
SERVING: Brunch, Lunch, Dinner
PRICE RANGE: $$
NEIGHBORHOOD: Roma Norte
This superb two-level restaurant and lounge bar
(overlooking the gorgeous fountains decorating **Plaza
Luis Cabrera**) and has a menu featuring Mexican
cuisine from all regions. Menu favorites include:
Oaxacan mole, cochinita pibil, and of course the tacos
and tortas. This place makes for great people-
watching as artists set up makeshift stalls to sell their
wares and the whole population flows by in a
continuous and colorful parade of humanity.

CAFÉ EL POPULAR RESTAURANTE
5 de Mayo, No. 50-52, Mexico City, 55 5518-6081
CUISINE: Cafe
DRINKS: No Booze
SERVING: 24 hours
PRICE RANGE: $$
NEIGHBORHOOD: Central Historic District
This 24-hour café offers great Mexican breakfast like
huevos rancheros or enchiladas verdes under a wood
beamed ceiling. Great coffees and pastries. If you're
lucky there will be live music.

CAFÉ NIN
Calle Havre 73, Juárez, Mexico, +52 55 9155 4805
www.cafenin.com.mx
CUISINE: Breakfast
DRINKS: No Booze
SERVING: Breakfast
PRICE RANGE: $$

NEIGHBORHOOD: Juárez

Great choice for breakfast and the most popular brunch spot in the area. Impressive selection of baked goods – everything from doughnuts to croissants and the best-ever guava cheese pastries. Delicious cappuccino. Nice small plates as well, like the avocado & squid ceviche.

CAFÉ PASSMAR

Calle Adolfo Prieto s/n Local 237, Mexico City, +52 55 5669 1994

No Website

CUISINE: Cafeteria/Coffeehouse

NEIGHBORHOOD: Benito Juárez

Just a coffeehouse that offers a full range of coffees beyond Starbucks presentation along with fruit smoothies, herbal teas, and frappes.

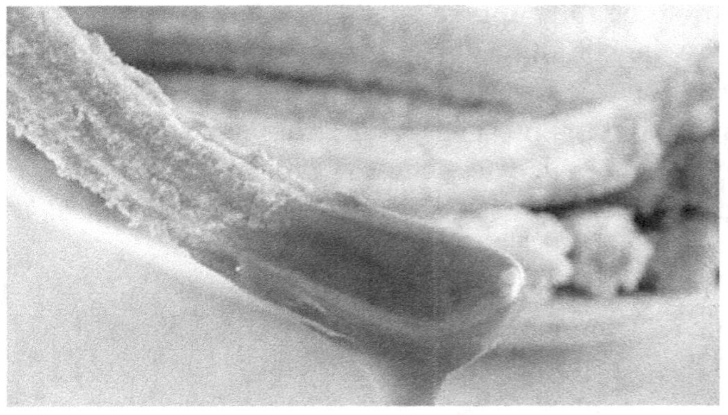

CHURRERÍA EL MORO

Several Locations (more listed on web site)

Eje Central Lázaro Cárdenas 42, Centro +52 55 5512 0896

Calle Río Lerma 167, Col. Cuauhtémoc + 52 55 5512 0896
Mercado Roma, Querétaro 225
Av. Michoacán 27, Col. Condesa
https://elmoro.mx/
CUISINE: Churros
DRINKS: No Booze
SERVING: 24 hours (some locations hours vary)
PRICE RANGE: $
NEIGHBORHOOD: Histórico, Centro / Roma Norte / Centro Sur / Condesa / Cuauhtémoc
Churros, churros, churros. Beautifully designed bakeries—light, bright and cheerful— (though the decor changes from one location to another) featuring churros, which is basically just plain dough fried and sugared. Originating in Portugal and Spain, churros are a mainstay snack here in Mexico and a lot of other Latin countries. They must be eaten when they're warm to be fully appreciated. Here at this bakery, where they do things the old-fashioned way, they make 'em to order, so you get fresh churros with a variety of toppings, everything from deep dark chocolate to dulce de leche. Try the churro ice cream sandwiches. Impressive selection of hot chocolates.

CONTRAMAR
Calle de Durango 200, Mexico City, +52 55 5514 9217
www.contramar.com.mx
CUISINE: Seafood
DRINKS: Full Bar
SERVING: Lunch, Dinner
PRICE RANGE: $$$

NEIGHBORHOOD: Condesa
This seafood restaurant is considered one of the chicest dining halls in the whole country, and not so much for its food, which is fine, but for the eclectic mix of artists, hipsters and trendy types it attracts. Blue and white color scheme highlights the high-ceilinged room. Best people-watching in the city. Has a great selection of dishes, including Tuna Tostadas, Oysters & pescado a la talla, Crab Cakes, and Spaghetti with Clams.

COOX HANAL
Calle Isabel la Catolica 83, Centro Histórico, Centro, 06090 Ciudad de México, CDMX,
+52 55 5709 3613
www.cooxhanal.com
CUISINE: Mexican
DRINKS: Full bar
SERVING: Lunch & Dinner
PRICE RANGE: $$$
NEIGHBORHOOD: Central Historic District
Popular eatery (since 1953) on the second floor offering authentic Yucatan fare like *poc chuc* (pork grilled after being marinated in orange juice). Other menu picks: Chamorro and Lime soup. Live music. This place was originally opened by boxer Raul Salazar, from Yucatan's capital, Merida.

DELIRIO

Ave. Monterrey 116-b, Mexico City, +52 55 5584 0870

www.delirio.mx

CUISINE: French/Deli

DRINKS: Beer & Wine Only

SERVING: Breakfast, Lunch & Dinner; closed Mon

PRICE RANGE: $$

NEIGHBORHOOD: Roma Norte

Great place to stop if you're looking for non-Mexican fare. Light dishes like focaccia.

DULCE PATRIA

Anatole France 100, Mexico City, +52 55 5282 1976
www.dulcepatria.mx/
CUISINE: Mexican
DRINKS: Full Bar
SERVING: Breakfast, Lunch
PRICE RANGE: $$$$
NEIGHBORHOOD: Polanco

Chef Martha Ortiz offers a menu of traditional Mexican cuisine with a modern twist. It's her innovative approach that has pushed her to the forefront of the "New Mexican" cuisine that's exploding all over the country (and abroad). This 90-seat eatery features two terraces inside the restaurant giving an outdoor feel. Begin with her ceviche. But also try her fabulous "sangritas" as a chaser after you down a shot of tequila.

EL CARDENAL

Palma 23, México, D.F., +52 55 5521 3080
www.restauranteelcardenal.com
CUISINE: Mexican

DRINKS: Full Bar
SERVING: Breakfast, Lunch, & Dinner
PRICE RANGE: $$
NEIGHBORHOOD: Centro Sur
Located in a beautiful old house, this popular eatery
serves authentic Mexican fare. Favorites: Quesadillas
with guac, and Chicken with nopales. Popular brunch
spot. If you're there for one of the best breakfast in
town, get the *huevos en caldo de frijol.*

EL FAROLITO

Altata 19, Col. Condesa, México, D.F., +52 55 5273
7297
https://elfarolito.com.mx/
CUISINE: Tacos
DRINKS: No Booze
SERVING: Lunch & Dinner
PRICE RANGE: $
NEIGHBORHOOD: Condesa
Delicious Mexican fare prepared right in front of you
at this decades-old spot with several locations. Try
the Faroladas de Bisteck (Pita bread with steak and
cheese). Nice selection of fruit juices.

EL HIDALGUENSE

Campeche 155, Mexico City, +52 55 5564 0538
No Website
CUISINE: Mexican
DRINKS: No Booze
SERVING: Open only 7 a.m. – 5 p.m. Fri - Sun
PRICE RANGE: $$
NEIGHBORHOOD: Roma Sur

A locals' favorite, this Mexican eatery offers a great selection of barbecue, meats, montalayo, and seafood. Authentic Mexican fare.

EL MAYOR

Républica de Argentina 15, Col. Centro, Mexico City, 52 55 5704 7580

www.restaurantelmayor.com.mx

CUISINE: Mexican
DRINKS: Full Bar
SERVING: Brunch, Lunch
PRICE RANGE: $$
NEIGHBORHOOD: Centro Histórico

Located on the top floor above a bookstore, this modern restaurant offers a menu of Mexican favorites and European-influenced fusion dishes. This is also a great place for brunch. There's a rooftop bar that overlooks the ruins of the Aztec city.

EL TURIX

Emilio Castelar, 212, Mexico City, 52 55 5280 6449
CUISINE: Mexican
DRINKS: Beer & Wine
SERVING: Lunch, Dinner
PRICE RANGE: $
NEIGHBORHOOD: Colonia Polanco
Located in a dingy storefront, but the food is worth
the visit. There's an outdoor patio and a couple tables
inside. Menu favorites include Cochinita pibil (pork
slowly cooked with achiote that is a specialty of the
Yucatán) and Tamales.

EL VENADITO
Universidad 1701, Col. Chimalistac, México, D.F.,
+52 55 5661 9786
No Website
CUISINE: Tacos
DRINKS: Beer &Wine
SERVING: Lunch & Dinner
PRICE RANGE: $
NEIGHBORHOOD: Florida
For over 50 years this place has served typical
Mexican fare to lines of happy customers. Known for
their great Carnitas. Favorites: Enchiladas, tacos al
pastor and French toast dessert. Across the street you
can see the Chapel of San Jose del Atillo.

ENO
Francisco Petrarca 258, Mexico City, +52 55 5531
8535
www.eno.com.mx
CUISINE: Sandwiches
DRINKS: Beer & Wine Only
SERVING: Breakfast, Lunch & Dinner
PRICE RANGE: $$
NEIGHBORHOOD: Polanco
Casual eatery that specializes in sandwiches. Great
spot for breakfast or lunch. Seating is communal.
Favorites include the carnitas de atun (seared tuna)
sandwich.

FLOR DE LIS
Avenida Mazatlan 30, Condesa, Mexico City, 52 55
5211 0060
No Website

CUISINE: Mexican
DRINKS: Beer & Wine
SERVING: Dinner
PRICE RANGE: $
NEIGHBORHOOD: Condesa
If you're looking for tamales, this is your place. There's a nice variety including chicken, peppers, beef, mole, and sweet (fruit). The atmosphere is quaint but the food is solid. Menu favorites included the Chicken and tomato tamale wrapped in banana leaf.

FONDA MARGARITA

Adolfo Prieto 1364, Mexico City, +52 55 5559 6358
https://fondamargarita.com.mx/
CUISINE: Mexican
DRINKS: No Booze
SERVING: Breakfast, Lunch & Dinner
PRICE RANGE: $
NEIGHBORHOOD: Benito Juarez
Authentic Mexican cuisine typical of the region. Try the chicharrones in green sauce served with fresh tortillas and eggs and beans. Very few vegetarian options. Spanish speaking only.

HAVRE 77

Havre 77, Col. Juárez, México, D.F., 5208 1070
http://havre77.mx/
CUISINE: French-Mexican
DRINKS: No Booze
SERVING: Breakfast, Lunch; closed Mon & Tues
PRICE RANGE: $$$$
NEIGHBORHOOD: Juárez

Small eatery reminiscent of cafes in Paris. A perfect place to stop when you want a break from Mexican food. Favorites: Steak frites, Escargots du Jour and Laitue (salad with fresh tarragon). Delicious French pastries make this a nice stop early in the morning.

GUZINA OAXACA

Masaryk 513, Mexico City, +52 55 5282 1820
www.guzinaoaxaca.com
CUISINE: Mexican
DRINKS: Full bar
SERVING: Breakfast, Lunch & Dinner
PRICE RANGE: $$
NEIGHBORHOOD: Polanco
Chef Alejandro Ruíz recently opened this location of his acclaimed Oaxaca eatery serving contemporary Mexican fare. Here you'll get delicious homemade tortillas, tableside served Oaxacan salsa, and mole. Great choice for breakfast. Make reservations for this place.

LA BARRACA VALENCIANA

Centenario 91-C, Col. Del Carmen, Mexico City, +52
55 5658 1880
No Website
CUISINE: Spanish/Tapas/Small Plates
DRINKS: Beer & Wine Only
SERVING: Lunch & Dinner; closed Sun
PRICE RANGE: $$
NEIGHBORHOOD: Coyoacán
Small eatery (only 12 tables) serving a menu of tapas
and small plates. Favorites include Squid Roman,
Grilled chicken breast and Chamorro veal. Specials
change weekly.

LA CASA DE LAS SIRENAS

Calle Republica de Guatemala No. 32 Centro
Histórico, Mexico City, +52 55 5704 3273
www.lacasadelassirenas.rest/

www.lacasadelassirenas.rest/
CUISINE: Continental
DRINKS: Full Bar
SERVING: Breakfast, Lunch, Dinner
PRICE RANGE: $$$
NEIGHBORHOOD: Centro Histórico (Central Historic)
This charming restaurant overlooks the Cathedral of Mexico City and the National Palace. Menu favorites include: Roast chicken and Rib Eye. Delicious desserts. The restaurant features a tequila salon with dozens of agave spirits and a rooftop with tables that looks into the cathedral's garden.

LA CASA DE TOÑO
Several Locations
Londres 144, + 52 55 5386 1125
https://lacasadetono.mx/
CUISINE: Mexican
DRINKS: Beer & Wine
SERVING: Open 24 hours (some vary)
PRICE RANGE: $
NEIGHBORHOOD: Juarez
Mexican diner open 24 hours. Very basic décor, nothing fancy. Large menu. Famous for its Pozole (which is a soup or stew with a base of hominy and mixed with meat (most often pork) and then finished off with seasonings and cabbage, lettuce, chili peppers, onion, garlic, radishes, avocado, or whatever they happen to decide that day. It's flavorful. But the menu is quite vast—enchiladas, quesadillas, cochinita tacos, flan, rice pudding. Favorites: Pozole and Horchata. Mexican beers.

LA CASTELLANA

AV Revolucion 1309 esq Corregidora, Mexico City,
+52 55 5593 5798
http://tortaslacastellana.com/revolucion_matriz.html
CUISINE: Mexican
DRINKS: Beer & Wine
SERVING: Lunch, Dinner
PRICE RANGE: $
Specializing in tortas, this is just one of five locations.
The tortas are made with crisp-crusted and light
bread, pickled jalapenos and a variety of fillings. And
cheap, cheap, cheap.

LA DOCENA OYSTER BAR

Av. Álvaro Obregón 31, Mexico City, +52 55 5208
0833
www.ladocena.com.mx
CUISINE: Seafood
DRINKS: Full bar

SERVING: Lunch & Dinner
PRICE RANGE: $$$
NEIGHBORHOOD: Roma Norte
Seafood eatery specializing in oysters and barbecue.
Favorite dish: Baby squid with garlic. Creative
selection of desserts. Reservations recommended.
English menu available.

LALO!
Calle Zacatecas 173, Mexico City, +52 55 5564 3388
www.eat-lalo.com
CUISINE: Breakfast/Pizza
DRINKS: Beer & Wine Only
SERVING: Breakfast, Lunch & Dinner; Lunch only
on Mon
PRICE RANGE: $$

NEIGHBORHOOD: Roma Norte
Chef Eduardo Garcia's casual eatery just across the
street from his more upscale eatery Maximo Bistrot.
Great choice for breakfast – have the French toast.
Amazing selection of pastries and house-made
yogurt. Dinner choices include dishes like freshly
made octopus with arugula.

LARDO

Agustín Melgar 6, Cuauhtemoc, Mexico City, +52 55
5211 7731
No Website
CUISINE: French
DRINKS: Full bar
SERVING: Lunch & Dinner
PRICE RANGE: $$
NEIGHBORHOOD: Condesa
Hip eatery with a menu of Mexican and international
cuisine. Great selection of seafood and seasonal
dishes. They will even make dishes to order. Nice
selection of wines.

LAS CAZUELAS DE LA ABUELA

Av San Jeronimo 630, Mexico City, +52 55 5683
8720
https://las-cazuelas-de-la-abuela.business.site
CUISINE: Mexican
DRINKS: Full Bar
SERVING: Dinner
PRICE RANGE: $
NEIGHBORHOOD: Pedregal
This family restaurant offers a menu of Mexican
cuisine with Poblano overtones. The menu features 25

different stews and delicious peneques – a deep-fried quesadilla with green and red pumpkin-seed sauce.

LIMOSNEROS

Av. Ignacio Allende 3, Col. Centro Histórico, +52 55 5521 5576

http://limosneros.com.mx/

CUISINE: Mexican

DRINKS: Full Bar

SERVING: Lunch & Dinner

PRICE RANGE: $$$

NEIGHBORHOOD: Centro Norte

Upscale eatery offering Mexican cuisine with an international twist. The interior walls look like they were patched together using ancient stones. These walls are high and very dramatic. Interesting clear glass light fixtures dangle delicately from the high ceiling. Pots and vases on a shelf look like someone had a field day at a potter's shop. The lighting at night makes the place quite romantic. Bottles behind the

bar are balanced (some of them precariously) on odd-
shaped stone shelves. Has a menu including tacos,
lamb, steak, Squid risotto and Crème Brule. My
favorites: the steak tacos. Nice wine list and tasty
cocktails.

LOS PANCHOS
Calle Tolstoi 9, Miguel Hidalgo, +52 55 5254 5430
www.lospanchos.mx
CUISINE: Mexican
DRINKS: Full bar
SERVING: Breakfast, Lunch & Dinner
PRICE RANGE: $$
NEIGHBORHOOD: Anzures
Great place for a family dinner.
Traditional Mexican eatery that's worth a try. Great
dishes and the steak here is exceptional (not your
typical American steak). Nice selection of desserts.

MAISON ARTEMISIA
Tonalá 23, Cuauhtémoc, Mexico City, +52 55 9036
3778
www.maisonartemisia.com
CUISINE: French
DRINKS: Full bar
SERVING: Lunch & Dinner; closed Sun
PRICE RANGE: $$$
NEIGHBORHOOD: Roma Norte
Upscale dining with an upstairs piano bar. Restaurant
offers a nice selection of seafood and beef. Favorites
include Grilled octopus and Short-rib ravioli. This

place is famous for its imported absinthe and absinthe-based cocktails.

MAXIMO BISTROT LOCAL

Av. Álvaro Obregón 65 Bis, Roma Nte., Cuauhtémoc, Mexico City, 52 55 5264 4291
www.maximobistrot.com.mx
CUISINE: Mexican, Italian, French
DRINKS: Wine
SERVING: Lunch, Dinner
PRICE RANGE: $$$$
NEIGHBORHOOD: Roma Norte
This rustic bistro, run by a young husband-and-wife team, offers a daily menu featuring ingredients found in the local markets. It has an open kitchen and has handwritten daily menus. Menu favorites include Lamb loin and Tartar of Steelhead. Reservations required.

MERCADO ROMA COYOACAN

Miguel Angel Quevedo 353, Mexico DF, 55 2155 9435
https://mrc.mercadoroma.com/
NEIGHBORHOOD: Coyoacán
Over 40 wildly diverse vendors occupy the 3 floors of this spectacular market, and a lot of them are eateries offering up authentic Mexican fare. While this is basically a collection of upscale food vendors that replicate the down-and-dirty street food you can find all over the city, in this place things are a little tidier, and the excitement stems from the fact that you can sample Mexican-fusion this or that, getting tastes

from the far corners of this country. You can get tacos from 9 different regions of the country. But also, elements of cuisine from around the world, all blended into Mexican cuisine. An Italian vendor serves tacos, but the taco is *piadina*, which is like a tortilla, but comes from Italy. Hundreds of surprising (and pleasing) combinations like this will enchant you. If you're on a short visit, this place ought to be a must, because you'll get to experience so much so fast.

MERENDERO LAS LUPITAS
Plaza Santa Catarina 4, Col. Del Carmen, México, D.F., +52 55 5554 3353
www.merenderolaslupitas.com.mx/ WEBSITE
DOWN AT PRESSTIME
CUISINE: Mexican
DRINKS: No Booze

SERVING: Breakfast, Lunch; closed Mon & Tues
PRICE RANGE: $$
NEIGHBORHOOD: Coyoacán
Family-run eatery offering authentic Northern
Mexican fare. Try the Atole (a corn-based drink
served hot). Favorites: Chimichangas, egg & bean
dishes and Flan.

MERO TORO
Calle Amsterdam 204, Mexico City, +52 55 5564
7799
www.merotoro.mx
CUISINE: Northern Mexican
DRINKS: Full Bar
SERVING: Dinner
PRICE RANGE: $$$
NEIGHBORHOOD: Condesa

Open since 2010, this eatery brings the surf-and-turf cuisine of Baja California to the Mexican highlands. Chef Jair Tellez created the expansive menu. Selections start with the small plate men featuring dishes like Ceviche ligero but don't forget the delicious main courses like Gently roasted grouper served on a bed of puréed cauliflower.

MOG
Frontera 168, Col. Roma, 52 55 5264 1629
CUISINE: Asian
DRINKS: Beer & Wine Only
SERVING: Lunch, Dinner
PRICE RANGE: $$
NEIGHBORHOOD: Roma Norte
This popular eatery offers a menu of sushi, Japanese style dishes and fusion. The bar serves a variety of Mexican and Japanese beers and sakes. Menu favorites include: Sushi rolls, Teriyaki Chicken and Yakimeshi. Desserts favorites include the green tea cake.

PASTELERÍA IDEAL
Several locations

16 de Septiembre No. 18, +52 55 5130 2970
Republic of Uruguay 74
Av. Hank González 773, Colonia Valle de Aragón
2nd. Sec.
https://www.pasteleriaideal.com.mx/
CUISINE: Bakery
DRINKS: No Booze
SERVING: 6:30 a.m. – 9:30 p.m.
PRICE RANGE: $
NEIGHBORHOOD: Centro Histórico de la Cdad.
Legendary bakery with endless aisles of breads,
cookies, croissants, cakes, and a variety of pastries
filled with ham & cheese, tuna, and other ingredients.
Worth a visit just to absorb the variety available. Plus,
it's a lot of fun to try pastry items you've never had
before. Eat in or take out. Cheap, too.

PASTELERIA LA GRAN VIA
Amsterdan 288-A, Mexico City, +52 55 5574 4008
www.pastelerialagranvia.com
CUISINE: Bakery/Specialty Grocery
NEIGHBORHOOD: Condesa
Popular bakery featuring a variety of breads, pastries, doughnuts, cakes and cookies. Great meringues and low-sugar options.

PUJOL
Tennyson 133, Mexico City, 52 55 5545 4111
www.pujol.com.mx
CUISINE: Mexican/Fusion
DRINKS: Full Bar
SERVING: Brunch, Lunch, Dinner
PRICE RANGE: $$$$
NEIGHBORHOOD: Polanco
With a reputation as one of the world's best restaurants (and hardest to get into with only a

baker's dozen tables), this Mexican eatery mixes modern (mostly French-inspired) and ancient culinary techniques. Prix-fix menu. Menu favorites include Fish ceviche taco and Fried pork belly. As an example of Chef Enrique Olvera's innovative culinary talents, I ordered tacos that had baby lamb, avocado-pera purée and the pungently aromatic herb, *hoja santa*. Delicious. Therefore, Olvera is Mexico's most famous chef.

QUINTONIL
Newton 55, Mexico City, +52 55 5280 2680
www.quintonil.com
CUISINE: Mexican
DRINKS: Full Bar
SERVING: Dinner
PRICE RANGE: $$$
NEIGHBORHOOD: Polanaco
This place takes traditional Mexican cuisine to the next level. Great margaritas and Mexican wines. Menu favorites include Swiss chard tamale with raison puree; delicate slices of *chilacayote* squash and charred tortillas are topped with mole; *Huauzontle*, which is something like broccoli, is fried and served with salsa and cheese from Chiapas.

RESTAURANTE NICOS
Av. Cuitlahuac 3102, Mexico City, +52 55 5396 7090
No Website
CUISINE: Mexican
DRINKS: Full bar
SERVING: Breakfast, Lunch & Dinner; closed Sun

PRICE RANGE: $$$
NEIGHBORHOOD: Clavería
Not your typical Mexican eatery, great menu of
"Nouvelle Mexican cuisine." Imaginative dishes and
what many say is the "best" guacamole in the world.
If you have a taste for sweets try the chocolate
mousse cake. Menu in Spanish but the waiters do a
good job of describing the dishes.
Good choice for breakfast.

ROKAI

Rio Ebro 87, Mexico City, +52 56 3035 4220
http://edokobayashi.com/index.php/rokai/
CUISINE: Japanese
DRINKS: Beer, Wine & Sake
SERVING: Lunch, Dinner; closed Sunday
PRICE RANGE: $
NEIGHBORHOOD: Cuauhtémoc
A favorite among locals and foodies, this small
Japanese eatery serves up famous dishes like Rokai,
mussels, sake, tuna, rib eye and duck, red snapper
with Himalayan salt and yuzu paste and Ensenada
Octopus sashimi. They also have a menu with nine or
ten courses –changing daily. They also have a real
standout menu item in their fried chicken. What
makes it different (and a delightful surprise for a
Virginia boy like me) is that it's marinated in sake.
The bar offers hot sake, green tea, Sapporo beer and
wine.

SUD777
Blvd. de la Luz 777, Col. Jardines del Pedregal,
México, D.F., +52 55 5568 4777
http://sud777.com.mx
CUISINE: Mexican
DRINKS: Full Bar
SERVING: Breakfast, Lunch, & Dinner
PRICE RANGE: $$$
NEIGHBORHOOD: Jardines del Pedregal
Great dining experience in a classic restaurant open
since 2008 that offers cutting edge innovative cuisine
while relying on traditional Mexican ingredients.
Updated, modern, but still somehow traditional. The
crisscrossing beams above give the place a modern
look, as vines weave in and out of nooks and
crannies. Light brown wooden tables mix with the
blacks and grays to highlight the intimate décor. The
chef swears he never uses any produce that's not
Mexican. (I believe him.) There is a tasting menu,
which I highly recommend. Be sure to get the wine
pairing, because this place has one of the best
selections of local Mexican wines to be had in the
city. Too many other upscale restaurants focus on
foreign labels. Favorites: Tuna tostada with soy,
Lechon pork, poblano chiles, Cotija cheese, a foie
gras that's made locally and Crab ceviche. (There
also a super good sushi bar, **Kokeshi**, tucked away
inside this place.)

TABERNA DEL LEON
Altamirano 46, Col.Tizapán San Ángel, 01000
México, D.F., +52 55 5616 2110
www.tabernadelleon.rest

CUISINE: Mexican gourmet
DRINKS: Full bar
SERVING: Lunch & Dinner
PRICE RANGE: $$$$
NEIGHBORHOOD: San Angel
Beautiful upscale though casual eatery offering an exceptional dining experience. Favorites: Pork chop with Brussel sprouts and Foie gras; *robalo a los tres chiles* (bass cooked with a three-pepper chili sauce). Excellent desserts like Chocolate cake served with raspberry ice cream.

TACOS DON JUAN
Atlixco 42, 06760 México, D.F., +52 55 5286 0816
No Website
CUISINE: Tacos
DRINKS: No Booze
SERVING: Lunch only
PRICE RANGE: $
NEIGHBORHOOD: La Condesa
Authentic hole-in-the-wall joint offering a rotating menu of fresh tacos. On Sunday, for instance, they'll serve tacos with *bistec con longaniza* (beef with sausage meat) topped off with a dollop of beans; on Friday or Saturday, you'll get *carnitas* (deep-fried pork). It doesn't matter what day you go, though, because every day the tacos are great, which accounts for the lines and why they've been here for so many years. Order at the counter – no inside seating, just outside.

TACOS EL HUEQUITO
Several Locations
Ayuntamiento 21, +52 55 5518 3313
Bolívar 58, Centro
Bajo Puente, Local 4 Esq. Juan Escutia, Col.,
Condesa
www.elhuequito.mx/
CUISINE: Mexican
DRINKS: No Booze
SERVING: Breakfast, Lunch, and Dinner
PRICE RANGE: $
NEIGHBORHOOD: Colonia Centro / Condesa
Taco stand located on a side street. Menu includes a
variety of salsas and sauces for your tacos. But there's
more to the menu—Gringas, Burritos, Nopalitos,
Arabs, Aztec Soup, Corn Quesadillas (tasty). Food is
served through a small window. Several locations
throughout the Central District, some with more
generous seating available than the little hole in the
wall I generally frequent.

TACOS MANOLO

Luz Saviñón 1305 (bet. Anaxágoras and Cauhtémoc),
Mexico City, +52 55 7095 8071
No Website
CUISINE: Mexican
DRINKS:
SERVING: Lunch, Dinner
PRICE RANGE: $$
NEIGHBORHOOD: Colonia Del Valle
This busy stand is all about tacos. Try the classic
Manolo, chopped bistec with onion and bacon.

TAQUERIA EL CALIFA

Altata 22, Mexico City, +52 55 5271 6285
www.elcalifa.com.mx
CUISINE: Mexican
DRINKS: Beer & Wine
SERVING: Dinner
PRICE RANGE: $$
NEIGHBORHOOD: Condesa

A popular taqueria with traditional favorites like the chicharon de queso and the Gaona conqueso.

TAQUERIA EL PROGRESO
Calle Maestro Antonio Caso 30, Col. Tabacalera, +52 55 5546 4700
No Website
CUISINE: Tacos
DRINKS: No Booze
SERVING: Breakfast, Lunch; closed Mon & Tues
PRICE RANGE: $
NEIGHBORHOOD: Tabacalera
Tacos at this great little sidewalk café are served with a variety of meats and lots of toppings including mashed potatoes, beans, cactus, manzanita peppers and onions. Cow head tacos served here (tacos de cabeza), as well as the excellent cow brain. (Check out the juice bar next door.)

TAQUERIA LOS COCUYOS
Calle Bolívar 56, Mexico City, 52 55 5518 4231
No Website
CUISINE: Tacos

DRINKS: Full Bar
SERVING: Lunch, Dinner
PRICE RANGE: $
NEIGHBORHOOD: Centro
This little taqueria offers up an interesting menu of
tacos. Bright lights illuminate the different cuts of
meat in a huge pan jammed with God knows what.
You'd never stop at a place like this ordinarily. It's so
small, so cramped, so scary looking. But it's the
BEST. (The smell is so wonderful.) You tell them
what you want and they cut the meat to order to make
some of the best tacos you'll ever taste. And cheap,
cheap, cheap. You eat standing in the street. Menu
favorites include: Suadero (braised and seared beef)
and Beef tongue taco.

TETETLAN
Av. de Las Fuentes 180, Col. Jardines del Pedregal,
Ciudad de México, +52 55 5668 5335
https://tetetlan.com/restaurante/
CUISINE: Mexican
DRINKS: Full Bar
SERVING: Breakfast, Lunch, & Dinner
PRICE RANGE: $$
NEIGHBORHOOD: Pedregal
Located off the beaten path is this ultra-trendy eatery,
that uses many kinds of stone in its walls, rocks,
bricks, poured concrete. Lots of weird angles, nooks
and crannies. Completely charming. The name of this
place means "place of many stones." You'll love it.
They offer a menu of international and regional
cuisine, boasting that over 90% of what they use

comes from Mexico. Favorites: Roasted huitlacoche
(this is a fungus that grows on corn), dried crickets
with lemon and Tamales with hoja santa. Nice
selection of tequilas.

TORTAS EL CAPRICHO

Augusto Rodin, 407, Mexico City, +52 55 3330 3935
https://tortaselcapricho.com/
CUISINE: Mexican
DRINKS: Beer & Wine
SERVING: Lunch, Dinner
PRICE RANGE: $
NEIGHBORHOOD: Colonia Mixoac
This eatery, very popular among the locals,
specializes in tortas, large cake sandwiches, and
offers nearly 50 varieties.

BALTRA
Iztaccíhuatl 36D, Cuauhtemoc, Mexico City, +52 55
5264 1279
www.baltra.bar
NEIGHBORHOOD: Condesa
Casual bar that offers a unique selection of cocktails –
many created with tea leaves as one of the
ingredients. Great selection of liquors.
Great comfortable bar with unique cocktails,
knowledgeable bartenders and good design!

EL DEPÓSITO
Álvaro Obregón 21, Local 1, Mexico City, +52 55
5207 8152
www.eldeposito.com.mx

NEIGHBORHOOD: Condesa
This is part of a small chain of beer-bar-bottle shops
that offer a wide selection of over 160 beers. Here
you'll find a great selection of beer on tap, Mexican
micros, European imports, German beers and a few
Belgians. There's a terrace, TV, and free popcorn.

EL REAL UNDER
Monterey 80, Col. Roma, 52 55 5511 5475
http://theunder.org/real/
NEIGHBORHOOD: Condesa
Another happening dance club.

FIFTY MILS
Paseo de la Reforma 500, Col. Juárez, México, D.F.,
+52 55 5230 1818
www.fiftymils.com
NEIGHBORHOOD: Juárez
Amazing quaint bar located in the **Four Seasons
Hotel**. The Manhattan is their signature cocktail and
it's top-notch. The bartenders are pros. But look
closely at the "Creations" cocktail menu, which has

cocktails unique to this wonderful lounge. Like Ant Man, which uses mescal, ants, egg whites, avocado, hoja santa bitters, soda water & lemongrass syrup. And that's just one cocktail! Plenty more to keep you busy. Hungry? Try the bar snacks like Grilled octopus with pineapple. Since you're here at the Four Seasons, try out the main restaurant, **IL BECCO**, featuring superior cuisine from the Piedmont region and a wondrous Italian wine list that will raise an eyebrow or two.

LA HERMOSA HORTENSIA
Callejón de la Amargura 4, Plaza Garibaldi 4, 52-55-5529-7828
No Website
NEIGHBORHOOD: Centro Norte
Located on the far corner of the Plaza Garibaldi, this pulquería is a must-stop for visitors. It's a 77-year-old pulque bar that serves the lightly alcoholic Aztec drink, made from the maguey plant. The drink has the

color of milk and comes in flavors like strawberry and coconut. This bar is included in the Museos Vivos project (which highlights "Living Museums"- every day venues that have cultural and historic significance).

LA NACIONAL
Orizaba 161, Mexico City, +52 55 5264 3106
No Website
NEIGHBORHOOD: Roma Norte
More of a bar than a restaurant with a very long list of Mexican microbrews. Great local hangout.

LICORERIA LIMANTOUR
Alvaro Obregon 106, Mexico City, +52 55 5264 4122
www.limantour.tv
NEIGHBORHOOD: Roma Norte
Popular bar that has been awarded the title as being "one of the best 50 bars in the world." Impressive cocktail list. Menu of bar snacks available – fries served with 4 different sauces.

M.N. ROY
Mérida 186, San Luis Potosi, 52 55 6681 0348
NEIGHBORHGOOD: Roma
www.mnroyclub.com
MEMBERS ONLY! Emmanuel Picault opened this
club and named it after the Indian revolutionary and
founder of the Communist parties in both Mexico and
India. It's super cool and gorgeously designed. Had
throbbing house music late into the night. Dress to
impress. It's a slick crowd here, even though the
outside is designed to look like a simple ice cream
parlor with a door the color of pink carnations.

PULQUERIA LOS INSURGENTES
Ave. de los Insurgentes Sur 226, Mexico City, +52 55
5207 0917
No Website

NEIGHBORHOOD: Roma Norte
Typical dive bar with loud music and sawdust on the
floor. Multi-level bar including a dance floor. Menu
of bar snacks. Live music and DJs on weekends. They
serve flavored pulque -blended fresh juice mixed with
tequila.

TÍO PEPE

Av Independencia 26, +52 55 8044 5884
https://www.cantinatiopepe.com/?lang=en
PRICE RANGE: $$
NEIGHBORHOOD: Centro Poniente
Located in Chinatown area, this old cantina is a
locals' favorite. How they can stand the harsh
florescent lights pulsating a nasty white light right
above their heads is beyond me. It would be a lot
nicer if they'd turn off those damn lights or put in
something nicer with a dimmer switch. Maybe light a
candle? I should stop bitching because I somehow
always end up here one way or another. A nice
ornately carved back bar touting Hennessy Cognac

makes a stab providing some atmosphere. Simple menu of straight tequilas, brandies, rum and Cokes, and Fernets with soda. No food.

ANAHUACALLI MUSEUM
Museo 150, San Pablo Tepetlapa, Mexico City, +52
55 5719 7652
www.museoanahuacalli.org.mx
NEIGHBORHOOD: Coyoacán
Designed by Diego Rivera, this museum houses the
artist's quirky collection of over 60,000 pre-Hispanic
pieces. The museum is built out of black volcanic
stone and resembles a pyramid. The collection
includes funerary urns, masks, and sculptures from
the ancient culture of Teotihuacan. Minimal
admission fee.

ANTIGUO COLEGIO DE SAN ILDEFONSO
Justo Sierra 16, Mexico City, +52 55 3602 0035
www.sanildefonso.org.mx
NEIGHOBORHOOD: Centro Norte
This 18th-century former Jesuit school reopened as a
museum and cultural center in 1992. The museum
features permanent and temporary art and
archeological exhibitions. Many come to view the
many murals painted on the walls by artists like José
Clemente Orozco, Fernando Leal, and Diego Rivera
(who also has a lot of works on display at the **Palacio
Nacional** a few blocks away). A gift shop is in the
patio of the Colegio Grande offering a selection of
museum publications, handcrafted jewelry, ceramics
and textiles.

CASA MUSEO LUIS BARRAGAN
General Francisco Ramirez 12, Mexico City, +52 55
8104 0688
www.casaluisbarragan.org
NEIGHBORHOOD: Daniel Garza
This is the former home of the great Mexican
Modernist Luis Barragán. The museum is a must-see
for lovers of architecture and exhibits Barragán's
work. It's often used by visiting architects. Modest
entrance fee.

CASTILLO DE CHAPULTEPEC
Bosque de Chapultepec, Mexico City, +52 55 7601
9811
https://mnh.inah.gob.mx/
NEIGHBORHOOD: Federal District
ADMISSION: Nominal fee, free on Sundays

Located on top of Chapultepec Hill, this is the only Royal Castle in North America. It was used to house the Mexican Emperor Maximilian I. This site was a

sacred place for Aztecs and the buildings were used as a Military Academy, an Imperial residence, a Presidential home and observatory. Today the hilltop castle houses the **Museo Nacional de Historia (National History Museum)**, with marble terraces, fountains and historic artifacts. You can climb up on foot (I did it one, but never again). It's worth the trip for the views alone. But the fountains, the marble floors and the historical exhibits make it even more special. Manet made a famous painting Maximilian's execution, and you can see how it was influenced by Goya's painting "The Third of May 1808" depicting the execution of Spanish soldiers resisting Napoleon's invasion of Spain in the Peninsular War.

CENTRO CULTURAL UNIVERSITARIO
(University Cultural Center)
Anillo Perif. Nte. 1695, Rinconada de La Azalea, Industrial los Belenes, +52 33 1377 5300
https://centrocultural.org.mx/
Located in a woodsy section of the university campus, this center is comprised of five theaters, including the Sala Nezahualcóyotl, home of the UNAM Philharmonic; the Teatro Alarcón, a drama stage; and the Sala Miguel Covarrubias, a contemporary dance venue. The cinema here shows Mexican and European films.

DAVID POMPA
Colima 264, Mexico City, +52 55 7261 8618
www.davidpompa.com
NEIGHBORHOOD: Roma Norte
Design studio of David Pompa selling high-end
lighting and furniture. A favorite among designers.

EAT MEXICO CULINARY TOURS
Sinaloa 149, Mexico City, +52 1 56 1899 5820
www.eat-mexico.com
NEIGHBORHOOD: Roma
Small private culinary tours of Mexico City. Get a
taste of what the locals eat. This tour takes you
through the streets of Central Mexico where you'll
sample street food, tacos and visit select markets.
You'll also get a history of the food you're eating.
Tours led by local, bilingual guides who share local
history and culinary tips. Six routes to choose from.
Tours are approximately 4 hours long.

ELENA GARRO CULTURAL CENTER
Calle Fernández Leal No. 43, Mexico City, +52 55
3003 4081/ +55 55 54-6198
www.educal.com.mx/elenagarro/
NEIGHBORHOOD: Coyoacán,
Beautiful cultural center designed my Mexican
architects Fernanda Canales and Arquitectura 911sc.
An old house has been transformed into a modern
looking cultural center with a library and series of
gardens and courtyards.

GOODBYE FOLK

Córdoba 55, Roma Nte., Mexico City, +52 55 5525
4109

www.goodbyefolk.com /
https://poplme.co/1V4Wh6Bu

NEIGHBORHOOD: Roma

Unique boutique that offers fashions and custom-
made shoes with an onsite hair salon.
Boutique. hairdresser, shoes made to order, free to all
Mexico. Boutique, hair salon, custom made shoes. -
we ship all around the world. Fashions like jackets,
sweaters, and shirts all have a vintage feel.

HILARIO GALGUERA

Francisco Pimentel 3, Mexico City, +52 55 2121-
6902

www.galeriahilariogalguera.com/

NEIGHBORHOOD: San Rafael

Perfect place to catch up top-notch contemporary
Mexican artists' work, like Bosco Sodi and Daniel
Lezama. Also exhibits international artists like
Damien Hirst.

JARDÍN BOTÁNICO (Park)

Av. Paseo de la Reforma S/N, Mexico City + 52 55
5286 6519

www.chapultepec.org.mx/actividad/jardin-botanico

ADMISSSION: Free

NEIGHBORHOOD: University City

This park and garden highlights Mexico's plant
diversity. The park is divided into 4 sections that
reflect the country's different climate zones. One of
the highlights of the park is a greenhouse filled with

rare orchids, but as you stroll through the trails, you'll encounter volcanic rocks and see examples of cactuses and succulents that are endangered species. Closed on Mondays.

JUMEX MUSEUM
MUSEO JUMEX
Miguel de Cervantes Saavedra 303, 52 55 5395 2618
NEIGHBORHOOD: Granada
www.fundacionjumex.org
David Chipperfield designed the Jumex, which focuses on contemporary artwork. Opened November 2013. When I first saw this collection, it was called the Coleccion Jumex and was on view in an old juice factory a bit out of town where it was Latin America's largest privately held art collection. Think Cy Twombly, Pedro Reynes, etc. The whole thing makes a much better impression in the Chipperfield building.

KURIMANZUTTO GALLERY
Gob. Rafael Rebollar 94, Col. San Miguel Chapultepec, 52-55-5256-2408
www.kurimanzutto.com/en/
Though this gallery is known for representing the top Mexican artists working today, it also has an impressive roster of international artists. Gabriel Orozco, Damian Ortega, Daniel Guzman and Dr Lakra all exhibit their work here, as well as Rirkrit Tiravanija and Jimmie Durham, just to name a few of the more prominent names.

MERCADO DE XOCHIMILCO

Nuevo Leon, Colonia Xochimilco
Farmer's Market OPEN DAILY
NEIGHBORHOOD: Xochimilco
This open-air Farmer's Market offers great shopping
opportunities for farm-fresh produce and other items
like the city's best barbacoa de borrego (slow-cooked
lamb). The market is also a unique dining option with
a variety of Mexican dishes including barbeque,
quesadillas, tacos, stew, and pambazos.

METROPOLITAN CATHEDRAL

Plaza de la Constitución, Mexico City, +52 55 4165
4052
https://catedralmetropolitana.mx/
NEIGHBORHOOD: Central Historic District

Opened in 1813, this is one of the oldest and largest Roman Catholic cathedrals in the Americas. This cathedral also acts as the seat of the Roman Catholic Archdiocese of Mexico. You can go to the roof of this cathedral where the view is spectacular as it overlooks what's left of the ruins (in the Templo Mayor) of the Aztec city that once existed here. (That city was called Tenochtitlán—try saying that fast 5 times.) There's a bar and restaurant up here called **El Mayor**, so you can get a cool drink after the long climb up.

MUSEO CASA DE LEON TROTSKY
Ave. Rio Churubusco 410, Mexico City, +52 55 5658 8732
www.museocasadeleontrotsky.blogspot.com
NEIGHBORHOOD: Coyoacán
ADMISSION: Moderate fee
The house where exiled Russian leader Leon Trotsky spent his final days has been transformed into a museum. Looking more like a fortress than a home complete with turrets for armed guards, this site is the final resting place for one of the most important figures of the Russian Revolution.
All information in Spanish only. English guides available for groups of five or more with reservations.

MUSEO CASA DEL RISCO
Plaza de San Jacinto 15, Mexico City, +52 55 5616 2711
www.museocasadelrisco.org.mx
NEIGHBORHOOD: San Ángel
ADMISSION: Free

Founded in 1958, this Cultural Center exhibits
Mexican and European painting, sculpture, applied
arts, textile works, and art objects purchased by
politician Don Isidro Fabela. Revolving exhibitions
along with the permanent collection, a library and a
gift shop.

MUSEO DEL JUGUETE ANTIGUO MÉXICO
Dr. Olvera 15, Mexico City, 52 55 5558 2100
No Website
NEIGHBORHOOD: Doctores
This multistory museum and art space built originally
to house the collection of Roberto Shimizu. The
collection mainly consists of mass-produced toys like
Mexican action figures, German-made racecars, dolls
heads, game pieces and lucha libre wrestlers. Roberto
starting his collection in 1955 when he hoarded all his
toys. His son now runs this collection of 45,000 items

in a place next door to an auto-body shop just south
of downtown.

MUSEO DIEGO RIVERA ANAHUACALLI

Calle Museo 150, Mexico City, +52 5719 7652
www.museoanahuacalli.org.mx/en/
ADMISSION: Moderate fee
HOURS:11 a.m. – 5:30 p.m. Wed-Sun
Designed by Diego Rivera himself, this impressive
museum made of volcanic stone houses his collection
of pre-Columbian art. The collection includes nearly
50,000 pre-Hispanic art pieces. The second floor
features an exhibition room devoted to the works of
Diego Rivera.

MUSEO FRANZ MAYER

Av. Hidalgo 45, Centro Histórico, Guerrero, +52 55
5518 2266
https://franzmayer.org.mx
NEIGHBORHOOD: Historic District
ADMISSION: Moderate fee; Tuesdays Free
Occupies the old hospice of the San Juan de Dios
order, this museum is home to Latin America's
largest collection of decorative arts. The museum also
sponsors workshops and temporary exhibitions. Café
located in central garden courtyard.

MUSEO NACIONAL DE ANTROPOLOGIA

Av Paseo de la Reforma y Calzada Gandhi S/N,
Mexico City, +52 55 5553 6266
www.mna.inah.gob.mx
NEIGHBORHOOD: Polanco

This national museum is the most visited museum in Mexico. Here you'll find significant archaeological and anthropological artifacts from pre-Columbian Mexico. Standout pieces include: the Piedra del Sol (the Aztec calendar stone) and the 16th-century Aztec statue of Xochipilli. The museum features 23 rooms of exhibitions filled with pre-Columbian treasures. An eye-opening collection.

PALACIO NACIONAL
National Palace
Avenida Pino Suarez, Corregidora esquina Guatemala, Zócalo, 52 55 3688 1255/ +52 (55) 5286-1743 ext. 412322
www.hacienda.gob.mx/cultura/museo_virtual_pal_nac/shcp_mv.htm
Of the 150 museums you can visit in Mexico City, this perhaps ought to be your first stop. This building was begun in 1693. The Viceroys of New Spain lived here until the Revolution. They have the whole history of the country's rich cultural diversity on display in the numerous exhibits here. There are huge murals by Diego Rivera depicting the history of the

country dating from its pre-Columbian era down through the Mexican Revolution. There's a replica of the first Mexican Congress, Recinto Legislativo. They have English-speaking tour guides.

SOUMAYA MUSEUM
MUSEO SOUMAYA

Blvd. Miguel de Cervantes Saavedra 303, 52 55 1103 9800

www.soumaya.com.mx

NEIGHBORHOOD: Granada

Billionaire Carlos Slim (some years, he's richer than Microsoft's Bill Gates, other years he comes in second or third) put up the money for this great place, which recently moved into a $70 million building, which itself is worth the trip. The Soumaya has the largest collection of Rodin sculptures in Latin

America (including more than 350 works by Rodin alone, but that's just part of the 65,000 items Slim donated to the museum, which is named after his late wife). It's better on a weekday if you can manage it because it's less crowded.

SPANISH CULTURAL CENTER
Pasaje Cultural Guatemala 18 — Donceles 97, 55 5521 1925
https://ccemx.org/
This Spanish cultural center features art exhibitions, plays, and music events. (There's a permanent exhibit of pre-Columbian art and artifacts, as well as rotating exhibits.) On the weekend (Thurs-Sat) you can see live music (indie, electronic and rock bands) on the terrace of the bar-restaurant. In the 1990s, this old mansion was in ruins until the Spanish government saved it as a historic monument to the city. The center

hosts workshops, seminars, children's activities, cultural events and exhibitions.

CARLA FERNANDEZ

Av. Álvaro Obregón 200, Mexico City, +52 55 4216 3389

www.carlafernandez.com

NEIGHBORHOOD: Polanco

Carla Fernandez, one of Mexico's top designers, offers her fashions in this boutique. She's known for creating Taller Flora, a demi couture line with a distinct geometric style, co-designed by and using Mexican artisans. Her Pret-a-porter line is also available here. Her fashions have been featured in all the major fashion publications.

CHIC BY ACCIDENT

Orizaba 28, Colonia Roma Norte, México, 52 55
8117 1140
www.chicbyaccident.com/
NEIGHBORHOOD: Roma Norte
Designer Emmanuel Picault brings together an
exciting and very personal collection of artifacts from
different parts of Mexico—furniture, accessories, art
pieces, gift items—that will give you a new sense of
the richness of the cultural heritage of this country.

COLONIA ROMA

This is one of the older historic neighborhoods in
Mexico City that's now packed with shops,
boutiques, antique stores, bars and cafes offering a
dizzying array of merchandise, art and food. The
architectural style is a mix of Art Deco and
"Porfirian," a mishmash of styles from Europe
fashionable when President Porfirio Díaz was in

office. The main streets to focus on are Álvaro Obregón and Calle Colima.

DULCERIA DE CELAYA

5 de Mayo 39, Mexico City, +52 55 5521 1787
NO WEBSITE
NEIGHBORHOOD: Cuauhtémoc
Founded in 1874 and located in an Art Nouveau gem, this is a mecca for lovers of sweets. Here you'll find treats like candied pineapple, guava, and other exotic fruits along with almond paste, candied walnut rolls, and cajeta. Many of these traditional sweets can't be found anywhere else locally.

FABRICA SOCIAL

Cordoba 67 Interior 1, Colonia Roma, Mexico City,
+52 55 5535 3431
https://fabricasocial.mx/
NEIGHBORHOOD: Historic District
This organization promotes the work of female textile
artisans through mobile workshops. This is a great
way to bring cultural awareness to communities and
sell the work.

GALERÍA DANIEL LIEBSOHN

Londres 161-49, Plaza del Ángel, 52 55 5525 2050
www.liebsohn.com.mx
NEIGHBORHOOD: Juárez
In Daniel's excellent gallery you'll find Mexican and
European antiques mixed with Italian and American
vintage furniture from the 20th century: you may see
a 15th-century Flemish painting beside a lineal seat
by Frank Kyle next to a 19th-century Napoleon III-
style mirror. There's no other gallery like Daniel's in
Mexico City. He has the best taste.

MERCADO DE MEDELLÍN (MARKET MEDELLIN)

Roma Sur, Cuauhtémoc, Mexico City
NEIGHBORHOOD: Distrito Federal
This is a popular Farmers' Market, located on the corner of Medellin and Campeche, offering a variety of fresh produce, spices, fresh juices, whole pigs' heads, meat, and other fresh food items. You'll also find plants, flowers and other items sold in flea market style. This place will give you an idea of the kind of cultural shopping tradition that is being decimated by the arrival of the "supermercados," supermarkets. Closed Sundays.

MERCADO DE JAMAICA

Guillermo Prieto 45, Jamaica, Mexico, +52 55 5741 0002
https://mercadojamaica.com/

NEIGHBORHOOD: Jardín Balbuena
This is a huge flower market that will have your head spinning.

MERCADO DE SAN JUAN

Calle Ernesto Pugibet número 21, +52 55 2248 6633
https://lacocinadesanjuan.com.mx/mercado-san-juan
NEIGHBORHOOD: Centro Poniente
Chefs shop here for foods they later sell you in their restaurants. It's really a unique place where you can get exotic meats like crocodile, ostrich, lion, deer and exotic fruits and vegetables, sweets, spices, meats, cheeses and products it's impossible to find anywhere else. Probably, you're not there to buy meats and cheeses, but like me, you just want to mix with the local crowds. This is a scene unlike any other. (Great place to buy gift items.) Watch out for pickpockets.

PANADERÍA ROSETTA (Bakery)

Colima 166, Colonia Roma, Mexico City, 52 55 5533 7804
www.rosetta.com.mx/

NEIGHBORHOOD: Roma Norte
This small bakery offers a variety of classic Mexican
baked goods like pan de pulque conchas as well as
delicious croissants, and vegan muffins. The menu
also includes well-made espresso drinks, sandwiches
and house-made pâté.

SANGRE DE MI SANGRE

Orizaba 101, Mexico City, 52 55 5511 8599
www.sdemis.com
NEIGHBORHOOD: Roma Norte
Located in a bohemian neighborhood, this is a
celebration of art and beauty through Sangre de mi
Sangre's jewelry designed by Mariana Villarreal. She
has two lines and her jewelry has been featured in
Vogue, Harper's Bazaar, and Elle magazines.

THE SHOPS AT DOWNTOWN

Isabel La Católica 30, Mexico City
www.theshops.mx
NEIGHBORHOOD: Historic Center
Located in the courtyard of the stately colonial home
of the Counts of Miravalle, built originally in 1846, is
a collection of over 20 unique shops offering food,
crafts, culture and design. The building was saved in
1985 and converted into a commer   cial enterprise.

INDEX

9 798822 419421 6